T0160844

WE,
THE
ALMIGHTY
FIRES

ANNA ROSE WELCH

WE, THE ALMIGHTY FIRES

ALICE JAMES BOOKS
FARMINGTON, MAINE
www.alicejamesbooks.org

Alice James Books are published by Alice James Poetry Cooperative, Inc., an affiliate of
the University of Maine at Farmington.

Alice James Books
114 Prescott Street
Farmington, ME 04938
www.alicejamesbooks.org

Library of Congress Cataloging-in-Publication Data

Names: Welch, Anna Rose, author.
Title: We, the almighty fires / Anna Rose Welch.
Description: Farmington, ME : Alice James Books, [2018] | Includes
    bibliographical references.
Identifiers: LCCN 2017052412 (print) | LCCN 2017052618 (ebook) | ISBN
    9781938584794 (eBook) | ISBN 9781938584756 (pbk. : alk. paper)
Classification: LCC PS3623.E46214 (ebook) | LCC PS3623.E46214 A6 2018 (print)
    | DDC 811/.6--dc23
LC record available at https://lccn.loc.gov/2017052412

Alice James Books gratefully acknowledges support from individual donors, private
foundations, the University of Maine at Farmington, the National Endowment for the
Arts, and the Amazon Literary Partnership.

Cover art: "A Rose Garden" by Brooke Shaden, http://brookeshaden.com/

CONTENTS

I.

II.

III.

IV.

ACKNOWLEDGMENTS

My gratitude goes out to the editors of the following publications in which these poems originally appeared, sometimes in earlier forms:

491 Magazine: "Trauma"
Best New Poets 2014: "La Petite Mort"
Barrow Street: "The Book of the Heart"
Crab Orchard Review: "L'Appel du Vide"
Gingerbread House: "The Scriptures Tell Us These Are Ordinary Times"
Guernica: "This Is How You Beg"
Kenyon Review Online: "Ravishment"
Linebreak: "Story in Which I Am Renamed Saint"
Los Angeles Review of Books Quarterly Journal: "There Were Blessings Everywhere"
Rufous City Review: "Singing Bowl"
The Adroit Journal: "To the Knees"
The Ampersand Review: "Desire," "Genesis," and "Redemption"
The Journal: "After You Left" and "Noah's Wife"
The Paris-American: "As If out of Clay"
Tupelo Quarterly: "Bridle"

"This Is How You Beg" was reprinted in *Guernica: Annual 2014 #1.*

This book would not have been possible without the love and support of my family and friends. My heart goes out to those who have read, guided, and supported my voice and the evolution of these poems from the beginning, especially: Jennifer Chang, Larissa Szporluk, Eugene Gloria, Abigail Cloud, Christopher Bakken, Jessica Bixel, Erin Miller, LewEllyn Hallett, Mel Mickael, Suzanne Hodsden, Paul and Joy Morin, Eric and Jade Ramsey Schlich, M.K. Foster, Carly Joy Miller, Sarah Porter, Kirsten Dean, John Cox, and all those in my Bowling Green State and Allegheny College families.

I would also like to thank Carey Salerno and the editors at Alice James Books for giving this book a home amongst so many writers I've long admired.

Finally, to my parents: from the second you put a violin in my hands at the age of five, you taught me the value of a life in the arts. I cannot thank you enough for whole-heartedly encouraging me to always pursue what I love. This book is for you.

I

THIS IS HOW YOU BEG

With a trowel, chipping bit by bit at the garden.

You find a pair of canaries—your mother's—long buried,

fallen wild. Gone, every muscle, wing, and feather tying the body

together. In your hands, their skeletons like light

slumped over a windowsill, broken-necked.

According to scripture, all you need is faith the size of a claw

to command whatever has left you to return.

Be uprooted and planted here again

in this cage I've built for you, you should say. Open your arms

wide as if the hull of a long-lost ark were coming to shore itself

against you. So often your mouth feels like the sky

in a dark, buttoned-up gown. Remember, that female bird

wasn't built to sing either, in accordance with science.

Take her fibula and tibia, made perfect from perching.

Take the radius and ulna from her clipped wings and replace his

with hers. It should feel like you've rebuilt man

from woman's most essential parts. This must be how God felt

when he wrapped the rest of you around something as small

as a man's rib and expected it to give you life.

ANATOMY

Call it what you will:

The moon filling its pockmarks with theft.

The algid sea thrumming once-caulked ships.

A house with four chambers where people wander saying, *Oh*.

Two staircases, separated by a single wall, commiserating in the dark.

The body: a half-acre tomb.

GENESIS

You were woven from animal fur, from another woman's hair, from grasses long dead and golden. Always spun from something else. Like the nests left when winter comes. Picture the darkest place inside a man's body and you'll know what he lost to create you. You, darling dim shape, learn all the right prayers: *Blessed be the first loneliness. Blessed be the will that drew me forth, that drove my heels into clay.* You were born into this world on your back. On the ground where you lay is your small human-shaped mark: the entrance to a new mine. The workmen will enter you singing, lights strung to their foreheads. At your baptism, the pastor will cover your own forehead with coal dust and say, *From darkness you were born. To darkness you will return.*

TO THE KNEES

I lived from one small domestic transformation
to another. At night, the pond broke to take in the rain.
In the morning, I heard you gathering your shotgun
from the dark corner of the stairs, its long length
a well-kept treasure. It might be beautiful in your hands,
the way light bursts from it like a brief tulip. To think
this is the last thing something wild sees, or doesn't see,
before it ends. You: into the woods, and I: my morning prayers,
ending every sentence with *Amen,* which will always mean
May it be so, no matter how much I hate to plead.

SINGING BOWL

For Centralia, PA

i.

Like the beginning of all things,
it was tremendous—fire
trickling into the carbon caverns,
coal imbibing heat and light
beneath the streets and houses
in the town.

ii.

On your fingertips, a bowl
of seven different metals.
Hit the rim with a wooden mallet.
You are the only way
it will keep ringing.

iii.

Smoke rose from cracks in the pavement.
Rust-colored clouds blossomed over hills.
The flames were never visible above ground.

iv.

If the ringing fades,
find the center
of the bowl's base,
its heavy balance,
your fingers like roots
connected to a bulb.

v.

The ground began opening.

It took houses and yards.

It almost took people.

vi.

The bowl is filled
with humming.

Your hand does not stop
skirting these edges—

wrists, forearms, clavicle,
manubrium, sternum—

no longer empty, glowing.

vii.

The residents left behind
a highway ending in the middle of itself.
A mine entrance useless, towering.
House foundations: whorls
of stone and wood.
Abandoned cars in the outskirt woods.
The town cemetery.
The ribs of ancestors
kindling this interior burning.

ORIGINAL SIN

It won't just be witches who burn this time.

We are guilty of being too luminous, each of us

no better than a thieving moon turning

in our daily beds. At the judgment, we'll admit to it:

everything has hurt us at least once.

We did what was asked. We woke with two arms

and two legs: open cages for others to dart into,

and, finding themselves still free, flee from.

To be gone from is to be lost,

but we're descendants of those who burned the lost

to keep seeing the living. That holy lamp of the body

is just a phrase reserved for saints—those gently lit marble

things—incapable of making wastelands of each other.

Here now, we kneel. We, the almighty fires,

thunderous with light, just begging one another—

or whatever other angels shall come—

that it'll be a kind of love these flames will give.

ROUGH MUSIC

We sought God together like peasants
spinning ourselves silly at a country-dance.
We found the wall, the window,
the foot of the bed. Without clothes

you're evidence man was created
in the Lord's image. In my hip-high dress,
I'm the world's original wound still covered over.
Look at this world

we've built ourselves. Even the garden
can't help but burst open, poppies
exploding unapologetically from delicate stems—
think, *Saint Theresa in Ecstasy*.

Who could forget the sight of her heart being broken,
or the way the altar makes even you feel
both sacred and conquered. We, the patron saints
of unkempt cotton, of friction against a wall.

Anything could be our god here, even that
upset curtain, that something with wings
slamming headfirst into its reflection,
into the window, into itself.

RAVISHMENT

Over the trees, birds hang themselves from the sky.

In portraits, the Christ Child clutches sparrows like these

in his fist. Something this ordinary is supposed to represent my soul.

In your fist, a tangle of my hair the color of a finch.

With each tug, my skull understands rapture.

Somewhere, I know there's a hunter with astonishing red hands

tossing a heart aside like a broken clock. It leaves its brilliance behind

on his skin, on the snow like a scarlet ribbon torn from a gift.

This is how we decide who the hunter and who the hunted:

light. First there's the chase, then the blaze, then the taking.

Into the woods like marionettes, the man, the sudden doe.

The trees trembling to flee themselves. The moon's silver

holy and wide like the jaws of a trap. Love, so much love,

thrown over a shoulder, its legs tied together with cord.

STORY IN WHICH I AM RENAMED SAINT

It'd been so long since we'd touched, you thought I must've found God. I caught you in the dark watching a video: a piano on the curb letting itself be touched and touched, singing for any finger that asked. It only survived one night before men with sledgehammers shattered it to tinder, took away each metal part that sang. Each time I caught you watching this—your face glowing in the darkness of our bedroom—you told me you were learning acceptance. After all, this is the world we live in: man can be broken and made whole again. Woman with all her faults remains dismembered: body forever in pieces. *I understand why you wouldn't wish to risk that*, you said, leaving space in bed between us, but growing increasingly jealous of thunder because it alone could rouse me in the night. This is the God you imagined for me: a storm I had no choice but to wake for. Maybe our God is the same. In my head, he has dark hair and olive skin and is far from soft when he bites a crucifix on the back of my neck.

TRAUMA

Imagine the body: a Canopic jar
silent, waiting to be uncapped.

Inside, a red sea swirling around islands
banished to some dark center.

History claims organs are only recovered
by smashing what possesses them.

That the body when torn resonates
the way earth does during the separation

of land and peninsula out to sea.
This body opens easily and fills with light

at the thought of being seen.
There is just the slightest crack

of something giving way. As if gods
were responsible for tectonic movement.

REDEMPTION

You grew up memorizing legends like the one in which the Madonna grabbed a thief's arm when he robbed a church, as if to say, *Give it up: only a small part of you is necessary to save your whole.*

The monks, finding it impossible to pull the thief from the Madonna's grip, hung his newly separated arm from the vaulted ceiling. They'll say it was God's wish this be done to scare off future thieves, but who's to say, really. There are two separate gods: the one you were born into and the One you were born under.

You've heard a group of women once allowed men to make relics of their limbs so they could live and feel like saints. For a century, the forests were flanked by men bowing before ankles, earlobes, and wrists hung in the trees by locks of hair. If these fragments swayed in the wind, the men knew God was present. If these fragments remained still, they pushed them to make them move.

In bed, you hold fast to your elbows. Even though you're pretty sure you misinterpreted the story about the Madonna, and even though you made up that story about self-sacrificing women, you force your fingertips into the junction between bones, mercilessly locked in place. Hear something outside the window chanting, *Yes.*

AFTER YOU LEFT

I said fuck it and let another man name me his ship-
wreck; call my arms and legs masts
snapping apart in his wake.

For every piece I gave him, I demanded a secret
about the ocean. Outside my window,
an oak tossed its helicopters to the black roof.

He whispered: *Listen. Something's devouring the leaves.*
Like this, he said, searching my mouth until I tasted salt.
Like this, his palms said, sinking to my hipbones

and the oak's branches, swollen with wind, finished
their desperate scratching on the window.
Like this, he said again and again

and again his fingers forged riverbeds between mine,
and his breath came and went in the canals of my ear
like tides crossing each other, until all I could imagine

about ocean was that it once was still
water interrupted by something heavy
collapsing into it.

II

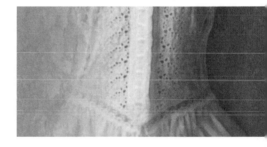

NOAH'S WIFE

I was that small, muscular knot at the base of the throat, rushing to untie itself.

There was nothing left of the earth to cling to, everything blue and hidden.

Earth and sky united at last.

There'd be no marriage in heaven, or so I'd heard,

just me: separate, whole.

I couldn't know that, one day, I'd be simplified into a tethered half,

that the remnants of sea would keep speaking long after dark:

So much of you was built for longing,

so little of you alone exists to fulfill it.

An unfaltering current assembled the shoreline. As a girl, I never listened to ocean and thought, this is how his mouth will sound on my skin—the hush of quartz learning water: a stifled longing for the heat it takes to become glass. I liked to cup my hands and wet them in waves big enough to swallow me, watch my small gatherings disappear before I could stand. How my palms were left, suddenly, filled only with sand. This is what I would become after the water had its way with me, or something else filled with breath.

To desire another is to lose your wits.
To lose your wits is to know God's hands.

I tried to convince myself of this
as the ark rose inch by inch,

as the loosed rain mistook
God's want as its own.

He wouldn't let me tear down the forest for a ship, but the lions needed to be brought into the new world. *Do it like this*, he said, and grabbed the struggling lion's neck to guide him like a mother does to her cubs. Teeth and jaws are less dangerous than woods. *If you're wounded, imagine each cut a mouth uttering praise*, he said, and I pictured myself being knocked down and separated into angry, red pieces by hungry jaws. Before those beasts, my prayers went like this: *If being undone brings me closer to You, God, then leave me whole and closer to Godless*, and the lions felt my hands and stilled, followed me obediently into my husband's boat. My hands have never been an agent of calm. Their touch would do everything but bring my husband to his knees. That was not how I pictured entering any sort of heaven.

Woman determines to study man as a book of the heavens.

Open him and find animals, trapped.

There: hyena on zebra.

There: an approaching snake.

If I, mother of these heavens—

The writers will leave this out of their book: that, long before there was God's favor, and long before the boat was coated in pitch, and long before he pulled me as wife from shore to water, I took my husband's arm and led him to the forest's edge. Before that kingdom of trees, I made him kneel and count each place he saw separate branches fastening together against a darkening sky. I held his head back—my fingers knots in his hair—until the day's falling forced itself down through every bare branch and disappeared, until the moon was covered in a fist of cloud and his entrance to the woods was blacked out and he was afraid he was going blind. This book will forget I put in my husband's chest everything he couldn't erase: the knowledge that the sweet light tangled inside the forest's thousand unions was not a blessing but a wound.

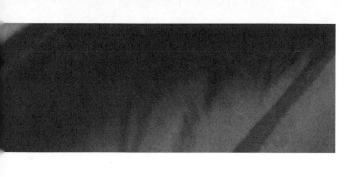

III

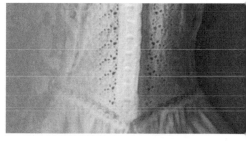

LA PETITE MORT

Affection had nothing to do with it.
When the water wanted something, it rose up
and took it like fathers do mothers.
Like boys do to girls to become men.

We left everything we didn't want on the banks:
once-practiced instruments, laceless shoes,
the feral newborns, blind and starved in a sack.
Committed everything to silt,
to downriver, to somewhere else entirely.

Kneeling in the reeds, we felt biblical.
Each thing was our own blue-eyed child,
and the reflections on the water's surface
made the branches above us look like out-of-reach crowns.

Like the current, we could get what we wanted
by lying down. We were the most beautiful we'd ever be
emerging from the reeds, dresses consecrated,
every stitch the color of clay.

ENVY OF DEEPER WATER

The remnant stalks of a pier are spread one after another:
a row of doorways inviting you to learn deeper water.

You'll hear one wave-crushed vowel after another,
the lost history of a wave shoaling, seducing

a clinker-built ship ashore. Inside its belly:
bones of a woman, thirteen horses, three dogs, and an ox.

Somewhere, the waves run in different directions.
Somewhere, the sea looks like a patchwork quilt thrown over the earth.

There was once a time no place could be left uncovered.
Sparrows leave the branch at the same time, write the shape of tide on sky.

And you're stuck between one doorway and the next, water to your knees,
wondering if it was really the ocean's repeated exhalation for the moon

that convinced women in legends to burn,
to be sent to deeper water with their masters' bodies.

AS IF OUT OF CLAY

From I don't know which rib I built my first man.
For him, I wrapped my wrists, the arches of my feet
in silk, tied back the unruly curtain of my hair.

I wore pearls like any other bride
and he bit them from my neck like any other man
tears the apple from its core. It's much too easy

to startle and run, to become the heroine
of a story told for centuries.
There are no stories about the women who settle.

Let me tell you one. I've counted my sins
like quarters; I've learned my worth,
how often I'd appear in the Bible as a lesson:

In this verse, woman finds playing God
takes the God from her, puts it in something else.
Build a commandment from this.

The first time water saved the earth, the chosen
animals wailed as if the Devil had finally come
for the leash of their throats.

Even our voices have never been our own.
I built a man from the chaos of my chest
but he was never my own.

If you must, label my book apocryphal.
These are the real lessons of creation—
we create only what we know will have dominion over us.

I knew his hands—the ones I gave him—
could mold me exquisite. Make me useless.
At least that's some kind of faith.

THE SCRIPTURES TELL US THESE ARE ORDINARY TIMES

The Bible said, *Let there be light,*
and there were men carrying lamps into the mines
and women scrubbing dust from porch steps.

The country—uncountable acreage—has been cracked open
like a rib cage and orchard trees are grappling with sky.
Watch them shift their roots.

On the branches, the weight of apples. Each fall,
a bright crush of red reminds us
hearts still work underground.

L'APPEL DU VIDE

Lately, I've been obsessed
with the concept of men
throwing themselves into the sea.

It's been proven
an excess of heat is to blame.
The sun begins and ends in water.

In Scandinavia, it's rumored
that groups of cows, perched on cliffs,
catch sight of the ocean miles away

and, longing to cross it,
fling themselves off the precipice
to reach the other side.

When men discover the tropics,
they are overwhelmed by natural light,
lapis lazuli above and below.

For centuries, the ocean has performed
the ritornelle of bodies
that recognize they're three-parts water.

Even Odysseus, claiming to hear women's voices,
tied himself to the mast of his boat
to keep his body from being taken first by waves.

HURRICANE MAP

A cartographical representation
of music's origins in the sea.
Stitched from the water to the shoreline:
thirty-five strands of numbers small enough
to be strings of eighth notes
thrown ashore by strange winds.
Black-ink crosses are planted on the shore,
each one a burial yard, a conglomeration
of shells shaped for the ear, and the skeletons
of seventy-five whales, each mistaken for a magnificent ship
left ravaged. The alternation of their ribs
an unheard sonic frequency
convincing piano makers
keys must always come from bone.

ARRIVING

There are fish in the net, the river says to the fisherman, the twist and pull of the net says to the fisherman. Into the ropes, the fish pour their armored bodies, saying they've forged the river to find its mouth and the mouth is now. When the head is severed and the fisherman holds the heart's mess in his palms, and the lips of the fish still move with singing, we'll admit there's always music in breath and scale and skin. When it's time for the disposal of the lungs the body calls my lungs, my lips, my tail, and when it's time for the washing of hands—my hands—the river will have no mercy except to lift all things toward sea.

THE BOOK OF THE HEART

Will you believe me if I say the opening of the ocean was the greatest
evolution for mankind?

> *I heard the water saying,* I want. *Just the water saying,* I want and
> want.

What happened after that?

> *My body learned to say the same thing.*

And after that?

> *I watched sparrows leave branches in V's, take the horizon like a*
> *thrust of tide over shore. I could hear them coming, each gasp of*
> *sparrows abandoning the forests for sea.*

What did their leaving sound like?

> *When it starts snowing and everyone buries themselves in blankets*
> *and looks out their windows as if it's the first and only time they've*
> *seen something lighter than water falling.*

What did their leaving sound like?

A shower being turned on and left to run. Expecting someone but staying empty.

What did their leaving really sound like?

A head of lettuce being undressed in someone's teeth.

Tell me something else that hurts.

In frescoes of The Last Judgment, *parades of men and women with bodies that look like mine march with open books on their chests and always, in the corner, a man, mouth open, speaks what we can never hear.*

What else?

Once, a lover watched me return from the small moments of ecstasy holding our desire in place. He said I was like a grand piano poised on a too-small windowsill—I just needed to let gravity erode my will to stay there above that beckoning street. I told him about how I saw a bride leap from a seventh-story window on her wedding day. The man who caught her didn't have to see her legs still choosing air. He wouldn't hear that part of her always opening and closing at her will.

When did you know things would have to be different?

When my body learned it couldn't forgive itself for him but forgave itself at the thought of being unrolled and pinned to the wall like a rediscovered map of eleventh-century Europe.

How does one rediscover a map?

Stand alone in front of a mirror and as you take off your shoes say: March of Spain to Aragon. *And as you take off your shirt say:* Salerno to Blois. *As you take off your pants:* Pamplona to Navarre.

How does one rediscover a map?

Just breathe in my ear because only then will we know how it feels when all water leaves the Mediterranean Sea to starve.

STORY IN WHICH I'M RENAMED EVE AND JUST DON'T GIVE A DAMN

It must've been exhausting to be God's first.
First demure virgin. First bride. First shut-up-and-stay-
in-the-garden-practicing-mysteriousness-wife.
Too many rules and just-let-it-be-so's.

In keeping with the Bible,
I practiced two-leggedness for a long time.
And then I didn't because I discovered four-leggedness
in a little room with the lights left on, and it wasn't magic,

and it wasn't Christ that brought my dress hissing to the floor—
He has so many brides already.
It was the curls sprung wild from another man's head.
The rain rattling the windows in warning.

Simple woman, simple woman, I could hear those syllables
in the shutters or maybe in his touch,
which was a different storm born to wear itself out
and take him away, gone.

What a blessing, to be so simple. To realize desire
is as much a purpose as anything else.
To be fallen, to be bare, to be an untied shock
of lightning in the center of a man's room.

THERE WERE BLESSINGS EVERYWHERE

The man who wouldn't touch me during
or after. The insomnia.
The way my breath sounded leaving,
like teeth into the skin of a fruit.
In the dark I could be a shard of bone
rejecting its body. I'm stealing the light
from whatever still has light to give,
which means I wasn't made in the image
of a great darkness capable of swallowing everything.
My mouth is small. My neck can be bent back
like an improperly struck match. Bless me.
Nothing I've built to worship is merciful enough.

DESIRE

This is how it is: the smallest body wracked
with song. Picture a stained-glass window shattering
to let loose hymns. I've never had the courage
to shatter anything. Sometimes, a rabbit's heart explodes
in its chest. Scientists say this is caused by too much fear
and too little body. But there's nothing small about a body
that took a crash from inside the forest and kept it.

SOURCE

In this land of disappointed miners, a river glows
with sulfur, the only remnant of the mines.
It repeats, *This is me. In case you've forgotten. This is me.*

The town church bells say the same thing
in four separate voices: *In case—me—you've forgotten—
me—this is—*. Once, a fugue of rocks

downriver drew a group of men.
They believed the ringing was inside the land
and so spent their lives disappearing into the earth

to find its source. Kneeling at a creek's edge,
children mine through the stones for a reason.
For the pebble that's almost clear,

for the softened lip of a broken bottle. Somewhere
someone threw part of themselves into water
and learned a new language in wreckage.

BRIDLE

You have a stampede of horses trapped inside you,
the doctors say, the scientists say.

They want to cut me open. Extract the Lipizzaner stallions
then sew me up right and decent.

I tell them there was a man. That he buckled a saddle to each ventricle,
turned, and ran, and didn't look back. That I let him.

They say: *If only you'd been the most beautiful thing.*
If only you'd been something certain, like a hoof striking shale.

I could argue. Say prayer can turn you into something new.
Had I gotten to my knees before him.

But there are some things a woman never speaks of.
Open wide, they say and I bare my teeth.

Open wide, and they push down on my tongue
with a piece of wood that weighs half as much as a page

ripped from some bible. We're all allotted our time to be holy.
A horse leaps above ground, becomes buttress,

becomes itself again. I fathom being both the rider and the bridled.
When they leap together it's considered majestic.

Without reins, it's just an animal lost to the wildest corners of a pasture. There is beauty there, too, or so I've heard,

where the tall grass says your name, continues to say and to say it
as you carry yourself through.

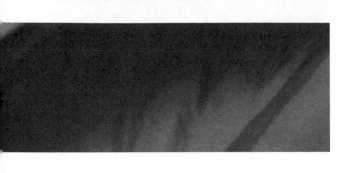

IV

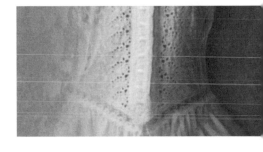

NOAH'S WOODS

I.

The make-up of a person is the functional sum total of all his past experiences.

In the beginning, the body was made of segments so irregular in shape and placement, it would challenge an expert juggler to keep them aligned. And yet somehow, there was a juggler: a man who knew to hold each of my segments briefly before letting go. There came and went my hippocampus. There my aorta, my jugular, my kidneys tied together like jump ropes. A pelvis to cradle it all passed from one hand to the other, and that's the part of me he chose to hold like my father did to my mother in the crush of bodies when they tossed each other around until there was me.

II.

The layers in the character may be compared to geological or archaeological strata which, similarly, are solidified history. A conflict...always leaves its traces in the character, in the form of a rigidity....Every muscular rigidity contains the history and meaning of its origin.

In Sunday School, we learned about the great ark, the one Noah demolished an entire forest to build. That's what it would take to keep from drowning, the Sunday School teacher told me as we glued popsicle sticks into rafts. We wouldn't be saved by the expansion of thorax, the contraction of diaphragm, intercostals, superior posterior serratus, and pectoralis minor. At the thought of water, there is no lifting the epiglottis; no expanding the larynx. In my head, the collapsing forest didn't go quietly and the animals preferred to drown. Noah clipped the orioles' wings to keep them from fleeing. He strangled two deer, his arms around their waists. He plucked earthworms from overthrown roots. I pictured each pair taken into the great ark: the necks of giraffes coming through the top deck; rabbit tails in the teeth of lions; sheep and anxious elephants in the same stall. In the darkest corner, the earthworms, cut in half by a cat's paw, kept moving further into the dark.

III.

[It] feels as if the pelvis were being drawn up toward the umbilicus as if by an external force. At the same time, the thighs remain still. It is extremely important to make the proper distinction between the natural vegetative movement of the pelvis and those other movements—the pushing out of the abdomen, the arched back, the whole trunk arching forward, reminiscent of the way a fish moves—that are a defense against [pleasure].

Your neck under my mouth was longer than I knew. In the years to follow I'd continue to think of it as the Cape of Good Hope—the one explorers and mapmakers misunderstood and drew as a peninsula large enough to separate oceans. Even though you knew how to touch someone other than yourself, your hands knew less than mine. Your first finger, your second finger tripped into the gorges of my hipbones. Somewhere inside my stomach, a glacier began its trek north, leaving only melting. My body could no longer be only my own, you said in few words, tongue scraping through my incisors, discovering the tips of my canines. When I distracted your blood, stilled it into pools at the base of your ear, you called them beautiful damages. Downstairs, my parents watched a crime drama, men extracting a woman's wrecked torso from the mouth of a tranquilized crocodile. No arms or legs. They washed up—beautiful—on the shores weeks later.

IV.

A living being develops a destructive impulse when it wants to destroy a source of danger.... The motive is not any primary pleasure in destruction, but the interest of the "life instinct"...to escape anxiety and to preserve the total ego. We destroy in a danger situation because we want to live and because we do not want to suffer anxiety.... The destructive impulse['s]... aim is not pleasure, although liberation from pain always is a pleasurable experience.

> Once, combining sun and mirror created a muscle of fire that set ships ablaze more than an arrow's shot away. Scientists have thought of stranger ways to explain how water came to hide the skeletons of ship-shaped forests. It wasn't the result I questioned. It took me forever to understand why those boats chose to leave the stillness of harbor for tide. How an armada could still burn while being swallowed by desperate water.

V.

Orgastic excitation…is experienced as a threat of physical destruction. Women fear "falling into the power of the man", being injured or exploded from within by him.

In the dark, all I could see of myself beyond you were my feet wrapped around each other, wrapped around you as if afraid to let go and enter the dark oblivion of the bed. Your ribs were content to remind mine I was somehow descended from them. And through all our contortions to reach one another, I thought only of a photograph: a pair of dancers in each other's arms. The ballerina, spineless, ribs connected to her partner's as if she were spilling from his chest. In front of his legs, hers. But it was almost impossible to tell whose were whose.

VI.

Women who previously had patiently endured living with an unloved man, who had suffered the sexual act as a "marital duty", were no longer able to do so. They went on strike, would have no more of it.

I saw two photographs of a dancer: one where her lover lay on the ground before her, his arm pressed to her breastbone. Here, saying good-bye meant pressing your lover's arm to your sternum. In the other photograph, the same woman sitting on a podium, legs stretched a mile before her. In shadow, her knee became an elbow and her shin a forearm and her foot—darkness packed between bruised toes—a hand reaching.

VII.

It soon became clear that orgastic potency and strong destructive or sadistic impulses are incompatible. One cannot want to give the partner sexual happiness and simultaneously want to destroy him or her.

This earth we lived on wasn't formed by a swift violence. In our flood, Noah had to plant the forest and wait for each tree to grow before sawing it down into a great ship. I read somewhere archaeologists found this ark nestled on a mountain in Turkey. They saw all the wooden beams, all the wooden walls. *Nothing human could've carried it to those heights*, they say. It had to be something mythic: a swelling of seas, a rapid drifting and disappearance of earth. What I know: the only reason the dove found the ship in the end was because it wasn't moving at all, base lodged on the summit, the ocean shifting around, giving the appearance of travel. All these words devoted to myth. We talked until our language carved us separate stalls.

VIII.

...In the current emotional regime, as we know, falling in love also commits us to merging. Meaning that unmerging, when this proves necessary, is ego-shattering and generally traumatic.

After you left, I twisted pine boughs and lights together on the walls. I hung a painting above what was our bed. A reproduction of Botticelli's *The Birth of Venus*—a woman born on the crest of sea, divine in every detail. You used to compare me to her when I'd come to you wet from the shower. I wanted to force you to sit and look at a picture buried in an art history book. A woman raises her white smock to her thighs. The lake startles around her calves as she proceeds into the water. Toward the end, this is what my body said to yours as you fought the sea of sheets and I wandered farther and farther toward the bedless edge.

IX.

Only when God and natural law are identical, can science and religion be reconciled.

Somewhere, an open mouth to a ceiling says, *God* and gets what it reaches for.

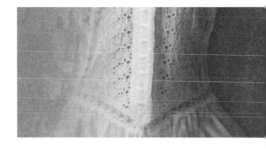

NOTES

The first line of "As If out of Clay" is quoted from an excerpt of *La Voile Noire* by Maria Le Hardouin, which appears in Simone de Beauvoir's *The Second Sex*, translated by Constance Borde and Sheila Malovany-Chevallier.

The italicized phrases beginning each section of "Noah's Woods" (excluding section VIII) are quoted (with some liberties taken) from Wilhelm Reich's book, *The Function of the Orgasm: Sex-Economic Problems of Biological Energy*, translated by Theodore P. Wolfe.

The first sentence in section I of "Noah's Woods" is taken from *Analysis of Human Motion: A Textbook in Kinesiology* by M. Gladys Scott.

The italicized phrase beginning section VIII in "Noah's Woods" is from *Against Love: A Polemic* by Laura Kipnis. Used by permission of Pantheon Books, an imprint of Knopf Doubleday Publishing Group, a division of Penguin Random House LLC. All rights reserved.

Recent Titles from Alice James Books

Alice James Books has been publishing poetry since 1973. The press was founded in Boston, Massachusetts as a cooperative wherein authors performed the day-to-day undertakings of the press. This collaborative element remains viable even today, as authors who publish with the press are also invited to become members of the editorial board and participate in editorial decisions at the press. The editorial board selects manuscripts for publication via the press's annual, national competition, the Alice James Award. AJB remains committed to its founders' original mission to support women poets, while expanding upon the scope to include poets of all genders, backgrounds, and stages of their careers. In keeping with our efforts to foster equity and inclusivity in publishing and the literary arts, AJB seeks out poets whose writing possesses the range, depth, and ability to cultivate empathy in our world and to dynamically push against silence. The press was named for Alice James, sister to William and Henry, whose extraordinary gift for writing went unrecognized during her lifetime.

Designed by Anna Reich | annareichdesign.com

Printed by McNaughton & Gunn